YOUR KNOWLEDGE HAS VALUE

Nitesh Polara

Effect of pre-cooling on post harvest life of Sapota (Manilkara achras (Mill) Fosberg) cv. Kalipatti

Post harvest life of sapota

GRIN Verlag

Bibliografische Information der Deutschen Nationalbibliothek:

Die Deutsche Bibliothek verzeichnet diese Publikation in der Deutschen National-
bibliografie; detaillierte bibliografische Daten sind im Internet über http://dnb.d-
nb.de/ abrufbar.

Imprint:

Copyright © 2013 GRIN Verlag GmbH
Druck und Bindung: Books on Demand GmbH, Norderstedt Germany
ISBN: 978-3-656-43520-4

This book at GRIN:

http://www.grin.com/en/e-book/214335/effect-of-pre-cooling-on-post-harvest-life-
of-sapota-manilkara-achras

GRIN - Your knowledge has value

Der GRIN Verlag publiziert seit 1998 wissenschaftliche Arbeiten von Studenten, Hochschullehrern und anderen Akademikern als eBook und gedrucktes Buch. Die Verlagswebsite www.grin.com ist die ideale Plattform zur Veröffentlichung von Hausarbeiten, Abschlussarbeiten, wissenschaftlichen Aufsätzen, Dissertationen und Fachbüchern.

Visit us on the internet:

http://www.grin.com/

http://www.facebook.com/grincom

http://www.twitter.com/grin_com

Effect of pre-cooling on post harvest life of Sapota (*Manilkara achras* (Mill) Fosberg) cv. Kalipatti

Makwana S.A., Polara N.D. and Viradiya R.R.

Department of Horticulture, College of Agriculture, Junagadh Agricultural University, Junagadh - 362 001 (Gujarat), India

ABSTRACT (Makwana Sachin)

An experiment was carried out to study effect of pre-cooling on post harvest life of Sapota (*Manilkara achras* (Mill) Fosberg) cv. Kalipatti at the Post Graduate Laboratory of the Department of Horticulture, Junagadh Agricultural University, Junagadh during the year 2010. The various pre-cooling treatments viz., control, pre-cooling at 6°C, pre-cooling at 8°C, pre-cooling at 10°C and pre-cooling at 12°C for 2 hours, 5 hours and 8 hours respectively with Completely Randomized Design with three repetition having total thirteen treatments. The results of the study indicated that mango fruits treated with different pre-cooling treatment showed lower and slower rate in physical and chemical changes than control fruits. The fruits treated with pre-cooling at 8°C for 8 hr proved to be most effective with respect to more number of days taken to ripe, longer shelf life, lower percentage of spoilage and higher percentage of marketable fruits. Lower physiological loss in weight and higher firmness of fruits. The treatment was also promising for slower increase in TSS, reducing sugar and total sugar, while slower decrease in ascorbic acid and acidity during storage. The organoleptic rating with regard to colour, taste and overall acceptability was also found significantly higher in pre-cooling at 8°C for 8 hr treated fruits.

INTRODUCTION

Sapota (*Manilkara achras* (Mill) Fosberg) is a tropical fruit, belongs to family Sapotaceae and is a native of Mexico and Central America. In India, the sapota crop is mainly cultivated for its fruits. The mature fruits are also used for making mixed jams and they provide a valuable source of raw material for the manufacture of industrial glucose, pectin and natural fruit jellies. They are also canned as slices. In India, sapota is cultivated in many states viz. Karnataka, Andhra Pradesh, Tamil Nadu, Gujarat,

Maharashtra etc. In Gujarat, it occupies an area of 27.4 thousand ha with a production of 272.6 lakh tones in 2009-10 (Anon., 2010). Sapota is an important fruit of tropical and subtropical region of the world. Sapota fruit comes under climacteric fruit category and it is very sensitive to cold storage (Laxminarayana, 1980).

The shelf life of sapota fruit is very short (2-3 days). After harvesting, if not handled properly, it becomes over mature within a day or two days at ambient temperature. The post harvest handling of the produce resulting in 20 to 30 per cent post harvest losses in fruits. The fruit is nutritious and fetches good returns. It suffers from a very poor shelf life associated with a rapid ripening in tropical atmosphere. The post harvest losses are high in tropical country like India range between 25 to 30 %. Therefore, there is a need to regulate it's ripening so as to improve its shelf life. For that purpose proper post harvest handling or operation must be required. Out of that pre-cooling is one of the primary post harvest operation. The main aim of pre-cooling is to remove the felid heat of the fruits and increase self life. So experiment was undertaken effect of study the effect of pre-cooling temperature and time ripening and quality bevariour of chiku fruits.

MATERIALS AND METHODS

The healthy, uniform in size and shape, free from any bruising and mechanical injured fruits of chiku cv. Kalipatti was selected and cleaned by washing under cold tap water then wiped with muslin cloth. Initial weight and girth of fruits were recorded and placed in different carats and were kept in pre-cooling chamber for different temperature (6, 8, 10 and 12 °C) and time (2, 5 and 8 hours) for pre- cooling. An experiment was conducted at the Post Graduate Laboratory of the Department of Horticulture, Junagadh Agricultural University, Junagadh during the year 2010 with Completely Randomized Design with three repetition having total thirteen treatments. After treatment fruits were kept in carats under open condition at room temperature (25 to 28°C). Two fruits from each repetition were randomly selected at a time and used for bio-chemical analysis as well as organoleptic test. The organoleptic evaluation for assessing the fruit colour, pulp colour, taste and overall acceptability was done by a panel of five judges by using 10 points scale system. Firmness of fruits was recorded by using Texture Analyser TA-X T2i, which measure firmness in kg. Texture Analyzer measure force in compression, probe having 5 mm diameter were

2

used for measuring firmness. The Analysis was done at five days interval and all the observation were recorded till the fruits were over ripe.

RESULTS AND DISCUSSION

The results showed that the physiological loss in weight of sapota fruits was significantly increased as storage period increased from 2nd to 8th days of storage (Table-2). The minimum physiological loss in weight was recorded in sapota fruits pre-cooled at 8°C temperatures for 8 hours (T_7). Moreover, other treatments comprising pre-cooling treatment also showed less physiological loss in weight as compared to control (T_1). Trivedi and Desai (2006) in guava reported that pre-cooling in shortest possible time after harvest had the minimum PLW in sapota.

The marketable fruit percentage decreased with increase in storage period. The fruits treated with pre-cooling increased the marketable fruit percentage with increase in storage period. In the initial stage fruits were hard, green and unmarketable but at later stages of storage the sapota fruit pre-cooled at 8 °C for 8 hours was found best for marketable fruits, and it gave firm, bright yellow color with good flavor fruits, as the concentrations of the treatment increased the colour and quality of fruits were deteriorated, as higher levels failed to ripen and restricted breakdown of chlorophyll and conversion of starch to sugar, the higher levels showed side effects on the fruits as black spots were observed on the outer surface. The results were confirmed with Gade and kedari (2003) and Raut and Pillai (2002) in sapota.

All the treatments consisting pre-cooling temperatures and periods extended shelf life of sapota fruits as compared to control (Table-8). The sapota fruits pre-cooled at 8 °C temperature for 8 hours (T_7) was recorded maximum (7.54 days) shelf life. The extension shelf life of sapota fruit through pre-cooling treatments might be due to the reduction in field heat in shortest possible time reduces moisture loss, restricts metabolic activities and respiratory activities, inhibit water loss and reduce ethylene production in fruits (Dewey, 1950 and Hardenberg et al., 1990). These results are in agreement with the results of Raut and Pillai (2002) Trivedi and Desai (2006). Anon., (1971) and Anon., (1991) were also seen similar trend in grape and mango, respectively.

The spoilage symptoms were minimum in fruits treated with pre-cooled at 8°C temperature for 8 hours (T_7). It reduced spoilage fruit percentage by prolonging keeping quality. The antisenescent properties help in maintaining the fruits on fresh condition during storage. The increased spoilage in hot water $50 \pm 2°C$ is due to activated enzymatic processes at higher temperature which enhanced the rate of various physiological and degradative processes also confirmed by Thangraj and Irulappan (1988) in mango and Ashwani Kumar and Dhawan (1995) in Dashehari.

The initiation of ripening process was found to be slower in sapota fruits pre-cooled at 8°C for 8 hours (T_7). Moreover, other pre-cooling treatments have also recorded delayed initiation of ripening process as compared to control. Pre-cooling treatments imposed immediately after the harvest inhibits the enzymatic activities and thereby reducing the rate of respiration and ethylene production which may leads to slower initiation of ripening process Hardenberg et al. (1990) and Dewey (1950). Similar findings were obtained by Vijaylakshmi et al. (2004) in sapota.

Maximum fruit firmness was recorded in control fruits (T_1). It was due to restriction of breakdown of chlorophyll and conversion of starch to sugar, the higher levels showed side effects on the fruits as black spots were observed on the outer surface. Whereas minimum firmness was recorded in T_7. Softening is largely due to breakdown of starch and other pectic polysaccharides in the pulp, thereby reducing cellular rigidity that were also quoted by Pantastico (1975) and Puttaraju and Reddy (1997) are in confirmation with present study.

Organoleptic characters of sapota like fruit colour, pulp colour and taste showed the highest score in the fruits when treated with pre-cooling at 8°C for 8 hours. Similar trend was recorded by Singh et al. (2000) in mango. The biochemical constituents of mango pulp can be correlated with organoleptic characters (Kapse, 1993). Similar trend was recorded by Ransing and Desai (2004), Oosthugse et al. (1995), Puttaraju and Reddy (1997), Galathia (2004) in different varieties of mango and Gade and kedari (2003) and Raut and Pillai (2002) in sapota and (Anon., 1978).

4

Biochemical parameters:

The total soluble solids of sapota fruits were not significantly affected due to different pre-cooling treatments on 2nd day after storage; while, onward it was remained significant up to 8th days after storage. The sapota fruit pre-cooled at 8°C temperature for 8 hours (T_7) was measured minimum total soluble solids after 4th day onwards up to 8th days of storage during experimental period. Slower increment in TSS may be due to pre-cooling immediately after the harvest reduces field heat from the fruit which restricts respiratory activities, inhibit water loss. Similar kind of result trend was also observed by Raut and Pillai (2002) in mango and Vijaylakshmi *et al.* (2004) in sapota.

In general, both reducing and total sugar showed increasing trend during storage. Reducing sugar and total sugar content was continuously increased during the storage period in Kalipatti sapota. This may be a consequence of release of sugar during starch hydrolysis during post-harvest storage and liberating reducing sugars (Kapse, 1993; Soule and Halton, 1955). The accumulation of reducing sugar and total sugar were slow and gradual in fruits stored in cold storage 8°C. The higher value of total sugar and reducing sugar in ambient stored fruits due to arrested respiration. Similar results are also reported by Dhemre and Waskar (2004) in mango fruit and Vijayalakshmi *et al.* (2004) in sapota fruit. It can also be observed that reducing sugars and total sugar content were reduced in the later period of storage. This may be due to their rapid utilization in respiration.

The acidity (%) of sapota fruits was not influenced under different pre-cooling treatments on 2nd day after storage and significant afterward up to 8th days of storage (Table- 22). On 4th to 8th days of storage, the maximum (0.20 %) acidity was recorded in sapota fruits pre-cooled at 8°C temperature for 8 hours (T_7). The treatments comprising pre-cooling treatments may be responsible for slower conversion of acids into sugars and utilization of acids during storage period (respiration) as compared to control (no pre-cooling). Meanwhile, after showing all the pre-cooling treatments, the sapota fruits pre-cooled at 8°C temperature for 8 hours recorded maximum acidity during storage period. This might be due to delayed ripening by pre-cooling treatments. These finding are in line with Vijaylakshmi *et al.* (2004) in sapota and Puttaraju and Reddy (1997) in mango.

Maximum ascorbic acid content was observed in pre-cooling 8°C for 8 hr. The pre-cooling treatment retards the ripening process and slows down the respiration of fruits and therefore higher level of ascorbic acid was observed. The results conformed to the findings of Singh *et al.* (2003) and Trivedi and Desai (2006) in guava fruit. The ascorbic acid content of fruits decreased gradually during storage in all the treatments, these all might have happened due to rapid conversion of ascorbic acid in to dehydro-ascorbic acid in the presence of enzyme ascorbinase with different level of oxidation in different treatments (Mapson, 1970). Among different storage condition had beneficial effect in reducing more ascorbic acid in cold storage 8°C fruit. This might be due to storage condition having been helpful to reduce the oxidation of ascorbic acid.

Conclusion

From the present study it is recommended that sapota fruits should be pre-cooled at 8°C temperature for 8 hours immediately after harvest is beneficial for increasing shelf life, quality and marketability.

Literature cited

Anonymous (1983). *Mango cultivation*, I.I.H.R., Banglore. I.C.A.R. pp.25.

Kapse, B. M. (1993). An integrated Approach to post-harvest handling of mango. (*Mangifera indica* L.) cultivar Kesar. Unpublished Ph.D. Thesis, G.A.U., S. K. Nagar.

Shanta Krishnamurthy, (1993). Handling and storage of fruits. Summer institute (I.C.A.R.) on Advances in Fruit production held at IIHR, Bangalore during Aug. 25-Sept. 13, 1993. pp. 496-505.

Anonymous, (2010). Director of Horticulture, Gujarat State, Gandhinagar.

Anonymous. (2010). Indian Horticulture Database, National Horticulture Board.

Krishnamurthy, S. and Rao, D. V. S. (2001).Status of post harvest management of fruits. *Indian J.Hort.*,**58** (1-2): 152.

Table 1: Effect of pre-cooling on physiological loss in weight of sapota fruits cv. Kalipatti during storage at ambient temperature

Treatments	Physiological loss in weight (%)				Marketable fruits (%)				Spoilage (%)			
	2nd day	4th day	6th day	8th day	2nd day	4th day	6th day	8th day	2nd day	4th day	6th day	8th day
T_1	1.02	7.86	14.30	0.00	61.71 (51.78)	45.56 (42.45)	36.82 (37.36)	24.63 (29.76)	12.14 (20.81)	25.49 (30.33)	35.21 (36.41)	40.50 (39.52)
T_2	0.85	2.25	6.43	11.06	63.76 (52.99)	64.50 (53.43)	69.64 (56.57)	66.84 (54.84)	0.00 (4.05)	19.08 (25.90)	29.84 (33.11)	41.64 (40.40)
T_3	0.85	2.54	6.57	10.75	62.74 (52.38)	65.68 (54.14)	76.03 (60.69)	72.27 (58.23)	9.89 (18.80)	17.24 (24.54)	24.04 (31.69)	28.46 (32.05)
T_4	0.89	2.54	6.73	11.35	69.51 (56.48)	60.89 (51.29)	46.66 (43.09)	39.29 (38.82)	11.14 (19.93)	21.90 (27.90)	24.67 (30.79)	35.08 (36.32)
T_5	0.83	2.51	6.41	11.13	68.46 (55.84)	61.00 (51.36)	52.00 (46.15)	48.69 (44.25)	10.45 (19.32)	20.99 (27.27)	33.60 (35.43)	38.14 (37.86)
T_6	0.84	2.34	6.66	11.50	75.49 (60.33)	67.50 (55.24)	57.35 (49.23)	55.51 (48.17)	0.00 (4.05)	20.17 (26.69)	26.90 (31.25)	41.50 (40.37)
T_7	0.85	2.04	6.07	10.56	79.46 (63.05)	68.50 (56.24)	72.57 (54.19)	79.69 (63.22)	0.00 (4.05)	16.30 (23.82)	21.14 (27.24)	25.81 (30.25)
T_8	0.89	2.98	7.11	11.79	71.14 (57.51)	58.97 (50.17)	58.94 (50.15)	49.28 (44.59)	3.86 (13.32)	21.78 (27.82)	32.52 (34.99)	34.41 (35.92)
T_9	0.90	2.76	6.86	11.42	59.97 (50.75)	62.22 (52.08)	67.65 (55.34)	65.40 (53.97)	3.31 (12.49)	17.16 (24.48)	27.19 (31.17)	29.33 (32.79)
T_{10}	0.91	2.55	7.32	11.65	70.21 (56.92)	62.08 (51.99)	61.94 (51.94)	51.71 (45.99)	3.78 (13.20)	21.47 (27.61)	33.00 (35.07)	42.31 (41.50)
T_{11}	0.88	2.57	6.54	11.42	68.12 (55.62)	61.89 (52.29)	62.74 (52.38)	65.68 (54.14)	4.52 (14.21)	18.14 (25.54)	30.00 (31.61)	34.02 (35.32)
T_{12}	0.91	3.39	6.36	11.44	66.06 (54.37)	63.00 (54.36)	64.50 (53.43)	60.89 (51.29)	3.42 (12.53)	20.67 (26.90)	29.98 (33.60)	34.40 (36.43)
T_{13}	0.95	2.65	5.31	11.67	69.36 (56.39)	62.04 (51.97)	65.68 (54.14)	61.00 (51.36)	0.00 (4.05)	22.75 (29.27)	32.02 (34.46)	33.21 (33.93)
S.Em.±	0.04	0.06	0.07	0.08	1.06	0.86	1.15	1.31	0.15	0.34	0.44	0.86
CD at 5%	NS	0.19	0.21	0.23	3.36	2.72	3.63	4.13	0.50	1.08	1.39	2.51
CV %	7.02	3.71	1.77	1.31	5.82	5.04	6.60	8.16	5.53	5.92	5.87	4.60

(Value) is transform value

Table 2: Effect of pre-cooling on physiological loss in weight of sapota fruits cv. Kalipatti during storage at ambient temperature

Treatments	Ripening (days)	Shelf life (Days)	Firmness (kg/cm²)					Fruit colour				Pulp colour			
			0 day	2nd day	4th day	6th day	8th day	2nd day	4th day	6th day	8th day	2nd day	4th day	6th day	8th day
T_1	3.75	5.12	7.41	6.98	4.13	3.66	0.42	5.88	7.78	5.56	7.58	7.07	6.91	7.31	5.43
T_2	4.74	7.14	7.42	6.89	4.73	4.29	0.75	6.07	7.49	5.73	7.62	6.98	8.06	6.99	6.95
T_3	4.93	6.70	7.57	6.18	4.52	3.88	0.79	6.74	7.39	7.21	5.35	7.36	7.82	7.30	6.61
T_4	5.09	6.78	7.23	6.60	4.27	3.83	0.82	6.56	7.71	7.72	6.50	7.29	7.59	7.14	6.85
T_5	4.59	6.94	7.35	6.40	4.23	3.70	0.54	7.40	8.45	6.60	6.72	7.48	7.71	6.44	6.87
T_6	4.81	7.19	7.35	6.62	4.27	4.44	0.75	6.42	8.45	5.75	6.45	6.73	7.92	6.40	6.26
T_7	5.24	7.54	7.13	6.54	4.40	4.63	0.84	8.43	9.20	8.63	8.05	8.28	8.64	8.67	7.67
T_8	4.62	6.71	7.19	6.05	4.80	3.91	0.80	6.29	7.81	7.27	5.54	6.94	8.00	7.84	6.77
T_9	4.42	6.95	7.24	6.88	4.53	4.06	0.51	6.32	7.51	5.95	5.32	6.80	7.54	7.57	6.41
T_{10}	4.61	5.25	7.35	6.75	5.46	4.49	0.93	6.75	8.47	6.76	5.14	7.36	7.44	7.19	6.54
T_{11}	4.00	6.50	7.38	6.97	4.19	4.38	0.51	6.39	7.89	8.05	5.47	6.49	7.42	7.51	6.80
T_{12}	4.81	6.36	7.24	6.81	4.62	4.20	0.49	6.94	8.30	7.62	5.12	6.67	7.64	6.30	6.63
T_{13}	4.61	5.96	7.46	6.40	4.56	4.24	0.56	6.50	7.73	7.36	5.33	6.98	7.81	7.03	6.81
S.Em. ±	0.10	0.06	0.14	0.20	0.07	0.06	0.02	0.17	0.19	0.14	0.10	0.16	0.19	0.23	0.25
CD at 5%	0.28	0.17	NS	NS	0.21	0.08	0.05	0.49	0.56	0.40	0.30	0.47	0.56	0.67	0.54
CV %	3.6	1.54	3.36	5.35	2.75	2.61	4.23	6.42	4.16	3.41	3.73	3.93	4.28	5.5	6.62

Table 3 : Effect of pre-cooling on organoleptic score* for fruit colour of sapota cv. Kalipatti during storage at ambient temperature

Treatments	Fruit taste				Overall acceptability				Total soluble solids (°Brix)					Reducing sugar (%)				
	2nd day	4th day	6th day	8th day	2nd day	4th day	6th day	8th day	0 day	2nd day	4th day	6th day	8th day	0 day	2nd day	4th day	6th day	8th day
T_1	6.12	7.33	7.71	5.38	6.89	8.29	8.33	0.00	16.73	16.71	18.58	21.72	24.81	7.72	8.75	9.34	10.44	10.79
T_2	6.99	6.86	8.11	6.38	5.85	7.49	8.96	0.00	16.63	16.74	18.94	22.04	25.79	7.71	8.37	9.28	10.48	10.72
T_3	6.51	6.75	8.19	6.74	5.51	7.41	8.85	7.91	16.50	16.48	18.67	21.50	25.90	7.72	8.72	9.22	10.46	10.77
T_4	6.60	7.14	7.28	6.11	5.16	7.16	8.64	7.89	16.63	16.63	19.64	22.91	26.36	7.74	8.77	9.40	10.46	10.83
T_5	6.95	6.94	7.80	6.48	7.90	9.03	9.93	5.78	16.50	16.48	19.57	22.85	26.41	7.72	8.73	9.34	10.45	10.88
T_6	6.46	7.09	7.76	6.19	7.95	9.14	9.86	0.00	16.50	16.48	19.28	22.28	25.69	7.64	8.69	9.41	10.51	10.86
T_7	8.21	8.54	9.42	7.67	8.28	8.17	9.84	9.38	16.50	16.48	22.16	24.91	26.78	8.08	9.10	9.90	10.92	11.28
T_8	6.58	7.38	8.11	5.88	6.57	8.04	9.49	8.09	16.43	16.32	19.68	22.37	26.05	7.74	8.77	9.44	10.48	10.81
T_9	7.44	6.56	8.34	6.99	6.00	7.72	9.16	9.32	16.73	16.70	19.60	22.41	25.68	7.68	8.72	9.38	10.53	10.88
T_{10}	6.98	7.18	7.61	6.42	7.57	8.81	9.66	0.00	16.57	16.57	19.87	22.78	26.09	7.70	8.75	9.36	10.46	10.83
T_{11}	6.34	7.78	6.98	5.76	6.52	7.98	9.40	8.21	16.73	16.83	19.74	22.34	25.65	7.75	8.75	9.42	10.48	10.81
T_{12}	6.13	7.26	7.66	5.54	7.24	8.55	9.55	5.88	16.63	16.89	19.29	22.65	26.15	7.72	8.73	9.44	10.47	10.77
T_{13}	7.26	7.17	7.70	6.56	6.94	7.64	9.12	6.49	16.52	16.63	19.54	22.35	24.86	7.72	8.74	9.45	10.60	10.78
S.Em. ±	0.25	0.20	0.25	0.23	0.08	0.04	0.03	0.03	0.16	0.15	0.13	0.13	0.16	0.07	0.08	0.07	0.05	0.07
CD at 5%	0.71	0.57	0.73	0.66	0.24	0.12	0.10	0.08	NS	NS	0.36	0.39	0.47	NS	0.23	0.20	0.15	0.21
CV %	6.23	4.74	5.48	5.25	2.13	0.88	0.62	0.94	1.54	1.52	1.11	1.02	1.07	1.63	1.55	1.26	0.83	1.10

*score out of 10 number.

Table 4: Effect of pre-cooling on total soluble solids of sapota fruits cv. Kalipatti during storage at ambient temperature

Treatments	Total sugar (%)					Acidity (%)					Ascorbic acid (mg/100 g of fresh pulp)				
	0 day	2nd day	4th day	6th day	8th day	0 day	2nd day	4th day	6th day	8th day	0 day	2nd day	4th day	6th day	8th day
T_1	6.26	9.71	10.79	11.85	12.83	0.228	0.23	0.13	0.08	0.00	10.79	10.40	9.09	8.07	6.06
T_2	6.35	9.84	10.80	11.84	12.69	0.232	0.23	0.19	0.13	0.08	11.18	10.50	9.23	8.63	6.34
T_3	6.29	9.75	10.72	11.83	12.82	0.237	0.23	0.17	0.13	0.08	11.20	10.53	9.38	8.54	6.35
T_4	6.88	9.83	10.73	11.84	12.85	0.225	0.23	0.19	0.13	0.07	11.39	10.45	9.24	8.43	6.54
T_5	6.67	9.73	10.64	11.85	12.79	0.229	0.23	0.19	0.14	0.08	10.91	10.42	9.35	8.64	6.74
T_6	6.56	9.69	10.71	11.82	12.81	0.231	0.23	0.19	0.13	0.08	11.24	10.42	9.38	8.44	6.28
T_7	6.44	10.41	11.27	12.41	13.42	0.222	0.22	0.20	0.14	0.09	11.57	11.21	10.03	9.94	7.32
T_8	6.54	9.71	10.77	11.83	12.84	0.223	0.23	0.19	0.13	0.08	11.32	10.44	9.41	8.48	6.56
T_9	6.59	9.84	10.82	11.87	12.82	0.227	0.23	0.19	0.13	0.08	11.28	10.49	9.38	8.29	6.24
T_{10}	6.44	9.65	10.70	11.84	12.78	0.232	0.23	0.18	0.13	0.07	11.47	10.51	9.24	8.93	6.28
T_{11}	6.49	9.88	10.63	11.87	12.76	0.229	0.23	0.18	0.12	0.08	11.39	10.49	9.17	8.48	6.40
T_{12}	6.65	9.74	10.73	11.78	12.77	0.231	0.21	0.18	0.13	0.08	11.15	10.58	9.20	8.57	6.63
T_{13}	6.78	9.74	10.72	11.81	12.82	0.224	0.23	0.18	0.14	0.08	11.38	10.43	9.38	8.64	6.51
S.Em. ±	0.13	0.10	0.08	0.07	0.08	0.007	0.004	0.004	0.003	0.002	0.15	0.10	0.14	0.24	0.17
CD at 5%	NS	0.30	0.23	0.21	0.24	NS	NS	0.013	0.007	0.005	NS	0.28	0.42	0.70	0.50
CV %	3.43	1.82	1.27	1.04	1.12	5.04	2.81	4.17	3.35	4.06	2.3	1.58	2.67	4.87	4.62

Eine paradoxe Handlungsaufforderung wird durch Missachtung befolgt und durch Befolgung missachtet

- Der Empfänger der paradoxen Mitteilung kann die Beziehungsstruktur nicht verlassen
- Es kann nicht über die Absurdität der paradoxen Handlungsaufforderung kommunizieren
- Obwohl sie sinnlos und widersprüchlich ist, ist sie pragmatische Realität: das Opfer kann nicht auf die Mitteilung reagieren
- Könne sich verfestigen: bereits Teile einer Doppelbindungssituation können typische Reaktionen des Opfers auslösen
- Der Sender der paradoxen Mitteilungen verbirgt sein Verhalten meist hinter der Maske der besteh Absichten
- Doppelbindungssituation kann eine <u>Annahme oder eine Nichtannahme</u> eben dieser hervorrufen. Die Annahme ist eine Belastungs-bzw. Stresssituation für das Opfer und daher auch eine pathogene Situation, was zur Ausbildung von Pathologien wie Schizophrenie, Hysterie, Phobien usw. führen kann. Die Nichtannahme führt zu einer Vermeidung der Doppelbindung durch <u>Metakommunikation</u> wie Humor oder Aussprache oder durch Flucht bzw. Trennung.
- Eine DB kann vermieden werden, wenn es dem Empfänger gelingt, dem Sender die Absurdität seiner Botschaft aufzuzeigen.

5. Stärken und Schwächen der Theorie

Stärken

- Die Krankheit oder das Problem wird beim Patienten als Symptom einer misslungenen Kommunikation gesehen, der Kranke ist so Symptomträger eins nicht funktionierenden bzw. fehlerhaft kommunizierenden Systems
- Probleme eines Menschen sind in erster Linie systembedingt
- Nicht er allein muss sein Verhalten ändern, sondern jeder der zu diesem krankmachenden System gehört

Schwächen

- Betriebt ebenso künstliche Isolierung, die, die, deren er Vorwirft, sie würden das Individuum außerhalb seines sozialen Systems betrachten: klammert Persönlichkeit und individuelles Verhalten zu sehr aus
- Beschränkt sich nur auf das Beobachtbare Verhalten: ist damit dem hier und jetzt verhaftet

6. Watzlawick formulierte 4 Schritte zur Problemlösung:

1. Zunächst muss das Problem definiert werden. Hierbei muss zwischen echten und Pseudoproblemen natürlich unterschieden werden.
2. Der zweite Schritt ist, die bisherigen Lösungsversuche zu untersuchen und zu sehen, ob die Probleme nicht durch Fehllösung entstanden sind.
3. Darauf folgt die Formulierung von Zielen bzw. Lösungen. In diesem Schritt sollte man Utopien und vage Lösungen natürlich nicht berücksichtigen.
4. Zu guter Letzt werden die Planungen durchgeführt.

- Die grundlegende Annahme war, dass das handeln psychisch kranker auf den ersten Blick völlig unverständlich wirkt, ihr Verhalten jedoch nach genauere Betrachtung den Regeln ihres Systems völlig angemessen ist
- Bildet nach B. die Grundlage der Schizophrenie und ist eine besonders destruktive Form paradoxer Handlungsanweisung
- W. sieht die DB nicht zwangsläufig als Ursache für Schizophrenie
- Aber auch er betont die krankmachende Wirkung n DB-Situationen
- Grundlage jeder DB-Situation sind paradoxe Kommunikationen

Paradoxien

- Paradoxe Mittelungen sind durch eine Widerspruch zwischen unvereinbaren Inhalten geprägt
- Eine paradoxe Handlungsanweisung ist ein widersprüchlicher Befehl, denn der Adressat unmöglich richtig ausführen kann

Doppelbindung

- Stellt eine Spezialfall der pragmatischen Paradoxie dar
- Kann entstehen aus der Unmöglichkeit, nicht zu kommunizieren oder aus sich widersprechenden Geboten
- Pragmatische Paradoxien, die widersprüchliche Handlungsanforderungen darstellen, können den Empfänger in eine unlösbare Situation bringen
- Eine besondere Bedeutung bekommen sie, wenn der Empfänger es sich nicht erlauben kann, nicht auf sie zu reagieren oder ihren Widerspruch aufzuzeigen
- Dies ist bei einer engen lebenswichtigen emotionalen Beziehung des Empfängers zum Sender der Fall (Familie, Freundschaft, Ehe)
- Eine DB kann vermieden werden, gelingt es dem Empfänger dem Sender die Absurdität seiner Botschaft aufzuzeigen
- Metakommunikation ist ein Weg die DB nicht annehmen zu müssen

Merkmale der DB

- Zwei oder mehr Personen interagieren miteinander, stehen zueinander in einer engen emotionalen lebenswichtigen Beziehung, diese ist meist komplementär. Der Sender der paradoxen Handlungsweisen wird als Täter oder Binder bezeichnet. Er ist in der Primärposition. Der Empfänger (Opfer) in der Sekundärposition: eine DBS kann durch Einwirkung einer oder mehrerer Personen entstehen
- Das Opfer macht die wiederholte Erfahrung der DB, sie besteht über einen längeren Zeitraum; hat daher den Charakter einer gewohnheitsmäßigen Erwartung für das Opfer

Störungen

- Situationen werden also immer subjektiv wahrgenommen und jeder Kommunikationsteilnehmer interpretiert die Abläufe nach seiner subjektiven Wahrnehmung
- Doch grade diese widersprüchlichen Interpunktionen sind Auslöser vieler Beziehungskonflikte
- W. geht davon aus, das Interpunktionskonflikte mit der tief verwurzelten und meist unerschütterlichen Überzeugung zu tun haben, dass es nur eine Wirklichkeit gibt: die Welt wie ich sie sehe. Und das jede Auffassung, die von meiner abweicht, ein Beweis für die Irrationalität des Betreffenden oder seine böswillige Verdrehung der Tatsachen ist
- Entgegen der subjektiven Wahrnehmung der einzelnen Kommunikationsteilnehmer hat menschliche Interaktion weder einen Anfang noch ein Ende: sie ist vielmehr kreisförmig: die Frage nach den Ursachen demnach müßig: denn hier ist jedes Verhalten Ursache und Wirkung
- Die unterschiedliche Interpunktion eines Kommunikationsablaufes führt zwangsläufig zu sich wiederholenden Verhaltensfolgen: gegenseitige Beschuldigungen und Schuldzuweisungen halten diesen interaktiven Kreisprozess aufrecht und hindern an der Lösung des Konflikts
- Wir sehen Konflikte im Alltag als linear an und gehen von einfachen Ursache-Wirkungs-Beziehungen aus, daher kommt es zu diesen Problemen

3. Die Selbsterfüllende Prophezeiung

- Phänomen im Bereich der Interpunktion
- Ist ein Erwartungsfehler: ein angenommenes Ereignis wird allein dadurch zur Wirklichkeit und bestätigt seine eigene Richtigkeit, dass es angenommen oder vorhergesagt wurde
- Diese Annahme musste nicht verbal übermittelt werden, es reicht aus, dass der Sender diese Annahme für sich hat: durch eine ursprünglich falsche Voraussage wird bewirkt, dass sich Personen dieser Prognose entsprechend verhalten und sie sich dadurch bewahrheitet
- Die SP hat also entgegen der kreisförmigen Kommunikationsabläufe einen Anfangspunkt: eine falsche Annahme einer Person: durch diese sie ihrer Umwelt ein gewisses Verhalten aufzwingt
- Ein Interpunktionsproblem besteht darin, dass die Person ihr Verhalten nicht als auslösend wahrnimmt, sondern nur als Reaktion auf das Verhalten anderer

4. Paradoxe Kommunikation und Doppelbindung

- Ursprünglich von Bateson und stellte einen neuen Ansatz zur Erklärung von Schizophrenie dar

- Sie kommunizieren auf gleicher Ebene: alles wird zurückgegeben: Komplimente, Schimpfwörter
- Komplementär: beide Partner haben hierarchisch unterschiedliche Positionen, Primärposition, Sekundärposition
- Bedeutet aber nicht gut oder schlecht, stark oder schwach
- Beruht auf einer privaten oder gesellschaftlichen Übereinkunft keiner der Partner zwingt dem anderen die komplementäre Beziehung auf, der eine verhält sich vielmehr so, dass die ein bestimmtes Verhalten des anderen voraussetzt bzw. verursacht
- Basieren auf sich gegenseitig ergänzenden Unterschiedlichkeiten
- Bei gesunden Beziehungen wirken beide Muster zusammen: abwechselnd oder auf verschiedenen Gebieten

Störungen

- Ergeben sich durch symmetrische Eskalation und starre Komplementarität
- SE: Bedürfnis eine bisschen gleicher als der andere zu sein: beide wetteifern um dieses Privileg: beginnt, wenn Beziehungssysteme ihre Stabilität verloren haben: Rivalitätskämpfe
- Extrem eskalierende Symmetrie führt zu einer Auflösung des Beziehungssystems durch Trennung, Scheidung, Totschlag, Selbstmord
- Starre Komplementarität: Beziehungsdefinition erstarrt, einer befindet sich immer in der Primär-, der andere in der Sekundärposition
- Stabilisiert sich dies, kann es zu Abhängigkeit, Unmündigkeit, Fremdbestimmung kommen; es kommt zu einer Entwertung der Selbstdefinition

3. Kommunikationsabläufe werden unterschiedlich strukturiert
- Für den unvoreingenommenen Beobachter ist Kommunikation ein ununterbrochener Austausch von Mitteilungen
- Doch jeder Kommunikationsteilnehmer legt ich unvermeidlich seine eigene Struktur und Gliederung der Abläufe zugrunde
- Diese Strukturierung nennt W. Interpunktion von Ereignisfolgen
- Interpunktion meint hier die Interpretation von Ursache und Wirkung
- Denn jeder Teilnehmer eines Streites legt den Beginn nach seiner eigenen Parteilichkeit jeder sieht sein Verhalten immer nur als Reaktion auf das des anderen
- Die Natur einer Beziehung ist folglich bedingt durch die Vorstellung von Kommunikationsabläufen, die jeder Partner der Situation zugrunde liegt

Bildquelle:
http://www.paulwatzlawick.de/images/
axiom3.jpg

4

- Da der Beziehungsaspekt dem Empfänger vermittelt, wie eine Kommunikation zu verstehen ist. bezeichnet man ihn auch als Metakommunikation
- Er kommentiert die Daten und gibt Hinweise auf ihre Interpretation: er beeinflusst den Empfänger somit stärker als der Inhaltsaspekt
- Außerdem bestimmt er diesen
- Inhaltsaspekt: was wird gesagt, verbale Vermittlung, sprachliche Kommunikation
- Beziehungsaspekt: wie soll es aufgefasst werden, wie wird es gesagt?: wird nonverbal vermittelt, nichtsprachliche Kommunikation: Gestik, Mimi, Tonfall, Körpersprachen

Störungen

- Stimmen Inhalts- und Beziehungsaspekt nicht überein ist die Kommunikation misslungen
- Bei einer Diskrepanz wird dem Beziehungsaspekt mehr glauben geschenkt

4. Kommunikation bedient sich digitaler und analoger Modalitäten
- Auf dem gebiet der menschlichen Kommunikation gibt es zwei Grundsätzlich verschiedene Weisen (Modalitäten) in denen etwas dargestellt oder mitgeteilt werden kann
- Digitale Kommunikation: durch Sprache, Inhaltsaspekt, beruht auf semantischen Übereinkommen, wird allerdings bedeutungslos, wenn die Beziehung zum zentralen Thema der Kommunikation wird
- Analoge Kommunikation: nicht sprachlich, Beziehungsaspekt, können mehrdeutig sein, besitzt eine größere Allgemeingültigkeit: bloßes hören einer fremden Sprache führt nicht zum verstehen, Gesten helfen dagegen dabei
- Digitale Kommunikation ist in zwischenmenschlichen Situationen immer von analoger begleitet

Störungen:

- Da analoge Mitteilung oft mehrdeutig sind, können sie vom Empfänger falsch verstanden werden
- Zu Kommunikationsstörungen kann es bei der Übersetzung zwischen beiden Arten kommen
- Besteht eine Diskrepanz zwischen analogem und digitalen Aspekt ist die Kommunikation misslungen

5. Kommunikation verläuft entweder symmetrisch oder komplementär
- Je nachdem ob die Beziehung zwischen den Partner auf Gleichheit oder Ungleichheit beruht
- Symmetrisch: Beziehungen beruhen auf Gleichgewicht: Partner streben nach Gleichgewicht und versuchen Unterschiede zwischen sich zu mindern, nehmen gleichrangige Positionen ein

1. Die Unmöglichkeit, nicht zu kommunizieren
2. Der Inhalts- und der Beziehungsaspekt der Kommunikation
3. Die Interpunktion der Kommunikationsabläufe (Jede Kommunikation ist Ursache und Wirkung)
4. Jede menschliche Kommunikation bedient sich digitaler und analoger Modalitäten
5. Kommunikation ist symmetrisch und komplementär

2. Axiome

1. Man kann nicht nicht kommunizieren

- Kommunikation findet nicht nur durch Worte statt, sondern auch durch nichtsprachliche Phänomene
- Jedes Verhalten hat Mitteilungscharakter: für Verhalten gibt es kein Gegenteil und keine Verneinung
- Auch wenn man sich von jemanden abwendet vermittelt man eine Botschaft, selbst, wenn man schweigt
- Alles hat Mitteilungscharakter

Störungen

- Zu Bsp.: Zugfahrt: Frau A sitzt mit verschränkten Armen im Abteil, Herr B. steigt zu und möchte sich unterhalten. Wenn er Frau A. versteht, wird er sie nicht ansprechen, tut er dies jedoch kann sie der Situation nicht physisch ausweichen aber sie kann auch nicht nicht kommunizieren: sie kann folgendes tunt:
    1. Sie kann die Kommunikation doch annehmen, gegen ihren Willen: widerwillige Annahme einer nichtgewollten K.
    2. Sie kann die K. abweisen
    3. Sie kann die K. entwerten: Man beraubt Aussage ihrer Bedeutung: Widersprüchlichkeit, häufiger Themenwechsel, Verdrehung von Tatsachen, absichtliches Missverstehen, Unkonzentriertheit; tut man dies gezielt und über längere Zeit entwertet man den Gesprächspartner selbst
    4. Sie kann Symptome vortäuschen um nicht kommuniziere zu müssen: Symptom als Kommunikation: man ist so nicht selbst verantwortlich für den Abbruch
    5. Bei allen vier Kommunikationsformen handelt es sich um misslungene Kommunikation, da die Botschaft von Frau A. nicht beachtet wurde

2. Jede Kommunikation hat eine Inhalts- und einen Beziehungsaspekt

- Inhaltsaspekt: vermittelt Infos und Daten
- Beziehungsaspekt: bestimmt, wie der Sender diese vom Empfänger verstanden haben möchte, er liefert also einen Hinweis darauf, wie der Sender die Beziehung zwischen sich und dem Empfänger versteht: in einer Mitteilung liegt eine persönliche Stellungnahme zum anderen
- Beziehungen werden selten bewusst und ausdrücklich definiert: meist indirekt über Gestik, Mimik, Tonfall, etc.

Kommunikationsmodelle/-theorien nach Paul Watzlawick

Inhalt

Watzlawick

- Ist gegenüber dem Sender-Empfänger –Modell dynamisch und interaktiv
- Erste Ansätze dieser Kommunikationstheorie gehen auf Bateson zurück:
- Er beschäftige sich mit der Reaktion von Menschen auf andere Menschen
- Nicht nur das Verhalten von A auf B ist wichtig, sondern auch dessen Verhalten auf A: soziale Kommunikation verläuft kreisförmig
- W. widmet sich in seinem Buch vorwiegend dem pragmatischen Aspekt der Kommunikation: dieser befasst sich mit Auswirkungen von Kommunikation auf das Verhalten der Kommunikationsteilnehmer
- Der begriff Kommunikation hat bei W. die gleiche Bedeutung wie zwischenmenschliches Verhalten: denn nicht nur Worte, auch nonverbale Signale üben Einfluss auf andere Teilnehmer aus
- Menschliche Interaktion versteht W. als ein System, das auf Regeln beruht; diese hat er in fünf Axiomen zusammengefasst
- W. geht davon aus, dass diese bei erfolgreicher Kommunikation berücksichtigt, bei gestörter nicht eingehalten werden
- Der Mensch beginnt vom ersten Tag an, diese Regeln zu lernen, obwohl diese Regeln selbst (das Kalkül der menschlichen Kommunikation) ihm kaum jemals bewusst werden
- Kommunikationsstörungen weisen also immer auf eine meist nicht bewusste Verletzung der Regeln im zwischenmenschlichen Bereich hin
- Auch psychische Probleme erklärt W. durch Kommunikationsstörungen zwischen dem Symptomträger und seiner sozialen Umwelt
- In der Metakommunikation sieht er ein Mittel um Störungen zu beheben

1. Regeln der Kommunikation nach Watzlawick

Nach Watzlawick besitzt Kommunikation ein pragmatisches Kalkül -ein formales System, in dem wir rechnen können- als Grundlage. Interaktion ist ein System, das auf Regeln beruht. Bei erfolgreicher Kommunikation werden diese Regeln eingehalten, bei gestörter nicht berücksichtigt. Diese Regeln menschlicher Interaktion hat er in fünf Axiomen zusammengefasst.

GRIN - Your knowledge has value

Der GRIN Verlag publiziert seit 1998 wissenschaftliche Arbeiten von Studenten, Hochschullehrern und anderen Akademikern als eBook und gedrucktes Buch. Die Verlagswebsite www.grin.com ist die ideale Plattform zur Veröffentlichung von Hausarbeiten, Abschlussarbeiten, wissenschaftlichen Aufsätzen, Dissertationen und Fachbüchern.

Besuchen Sie uns im Internet:

http://www.grin.com/

http://www.facebook.com/grincom

http://www.twitter.com/grin_com

Elisabeth Dölle

Die Kommunikationsmodelle und -theorien nach Paul Watzlawick. Ein Überblick

GRIN Verlag

Bibliografische Information der Deutschen Nationalbibliothek:

Die Deutsche Bibliothek verzeichnet diese Publikation in der Deutschen National-
bibliografie; detaillierte bibliografische Daten sind im Internet über http://dnb.d-
nb.de/ abrufbar.

Impressum:

Copyright © 2015 GRIN Verlag, Open Publishing GmbH
Druck und Bindung: Books on Demand GmbH, Norderstedt Germany
ISBN: 978-3-668-07207-7

Dieses Buch bei GRIN:

http://www.grin.com/de/e-book/308568/die-kommunikationsmodelle-und-theorien-
nach-paul-watzlawick-ein-ueberblick

BEI GRIN MACHT SICH IHR WISSEN BEZAHLT

- Wir veröffentlichen Ihre Hausarbeit, Bachelor- und Masterarbeit

- Ihr eigenes eBook und Buch - weltweit in allen wichtigen Shops

- Verdienen Sie an jedem Verkauf

Jetzt bei www.GRIN.com hochladen und kostenlos publizieren